Ten Poems
about Wine

ex libris

Candlestick Press

Published by:
Candlestick Press,
Diversity House, 72 Nottingham Road, Arnold, Nottingham NG5 6LF
www.candlestickpress.co.uk

Design and typesetting by Craig Twigg

Printed by Ratcliff & Roper Print Group, Nottinghamshire, UK

Selection and Introduction © Jonathan Davidson, 2023

Cover illustration © Jane Walker, 2023
www.janewalkerprintmaker.com

Candlestick Press monogram © Barbara Shaw, 2008

© Candlestick Press, 2023

ISBN 978 1 913627 22 5

Acknowledgements

The poems in this pamphlet are reprinted from the following books, all by
permission of the publishers listed unless stated otherwise. Every effort has been
made to trace the copyright holders of the poems published in this book. The
editor and publisher apologise if any material has been included without
permission, or without the appropriate acknowledgement, and would be glad to
be told of anyone who has not been consulted.

Thanks are due to all the copyright holders cited below for their kind permission.

Li Bai, first published at www.davidbowles.us on April 23, 2014. By kind
permission of the translator, David Bowles – Associate Professor of Literatures
and Cultural Studies at the University of Texas Rio Grande Valley. Jane
Commane, poem first published in this anthology. Wendy Cope, *Serious
Concerns* (Faber & Faber, 1992) by permission of the publisher and United
Agents. Jonathan Davidson, poem first published in this anthology. Gregory
Leadbetter, poem first published in this anthology. Matthew Stewart, an earlier
version of this poem was published in *The New European*, Issue Nº 215, October
2020. Emma Storr, poem first published in this anthology. Miriam Wei Wei Lo,
Cullen Wines Poetry Collection, (Margaret River Press, 2014) by kind permission
of the author.

All permissions cleared courtesy of Dr Suzanne Fairless-Aitken
c/o Swift Permissions swiftpermissions@gmail.com

Where poets are no longer living, their dates are given.

Contents

Introduction

The writer Robert Louis Stevenson said, "*Wine* is bottled *poetry*," and he was not wrong. While we don't know which came first, both involve the fermenting of rather everyday things – grapes, language – to produce something that can be sublime. And both are examples of human ingenuity and artistry.

Neither good wine nor good poetry are easily produced, and the magic hand of chance plays its part. The underlying rock and the soil in which a poem – and grapes – grow are important. The degree of wind and rain or sun and warmth, they play their part, as John Keats knew when he wrote of his "beaker of the warm South".

The making of poetry and the making of wine are only one half of the process. A wine is nothing if it is not drunk, and a poem unread is dead to the world. While the over-indulgence in poetry is not quite so concerning as imbibing rather too freely of the grape, there is a taste – a palate – to be developed in both cases.

A rough-hewn verse might please for a moment, but a truly wonderful poem can give pleasure for centuries. It demands a certain approach from the reader or listener. It may, as my own poem in this anthology suggests, have a "long finish". And to drink wine slowly over many years is to appreciate the subtleties on offer; the tone and cadences, the rhyme scheme, shall we say.

The poems laid down for you here in this little cellar of verse have been chosen for their wit and understanding. While they appreciate the relentless contrariness of the world, they remind us that to take a glass of wine now and then offers us a shaft of sunlight through the clouds. To read through a poem or two while doing so can do nothing but enrich that experience.

To those who enjoy good poetry and good wine, I raise a glass with – in John Keats' lovely phrase – "beaded bubbles winking at the brim".

Jonathan Davidson

The Vine

The wine of Love is music,
  And the feast of Love is song:
And when Love sits down to the banquet,
  Love sits long:

Sits long and arises drunken,
  But not with the feast and the wine;
He reeleth with his own heart,
  That great, rich Vine.

James Thomson (1700 – 1748)

La Vendimia

After peaches come to an end,
before olives start, labourers
from over a dozen countries

head for Villalejo vineyards
and stoop and rise and stoop and rise,
grafting through the cool of the night —

snipping bunches, loading baskets
and heaving grapes into trailers.
By dawn, tractors have queued and chugged

their way through the winery gates.
Alchemy's about to begin.
The sleeping town will be woken

to heady scents of cherries,
yeast and just-crushed rose petals
wafting from roof to pavement.

Matthew Stewart

From **Ode to a Nightingale**

  O, for a draught of vintage! that hath been
        Cool'd a long age in the deep-delv'd earth,
Tasting of Flora and the country-green,
        Dance, and Provençal song, and sunburnt mirth!
O, for a beaker of the warm South,
      Full of the true, the blushful Hippocrene,
          With beaded bubbles winking at the brim,
            And purple-stained mouth;
     That I might drink, and leave the world unseen,
        And with thee fade away into the forest dim:

John Keats (1795 – 1821)

Cullen Late Harvest
Semillon 2012

I open the pantry door
and find, to my surprise,
that the children have left
three squares of chocolate
wrapped in golden foil
in the corner of a zip-lock bag.

        They are as sweet
        as the bottle of wine
        you left in my bicycle basket.

Miriam Wei Wei Lo

Tasting Notes

A found poem from Majestic Wine

The Customer Happiness Team
is available: do I want wine
tasting of roundness, or fruits

that linger: plum, blueberry and lime?
They promise toasted spices
marrying passion with vibrancy.

The Happiness Team propose
that my excellent choice
of a Marlborough Sauv Blanc

can be shared with mature
goat cheese, friends, or drunk
simply on its own.

I admire the Kiwi label,
the reassuring 13%, the click
as I unscrew the cap.

They are so right: I *can* drink
on my own. I am cut grass,
light-bodied, off-dry.

Emma Storr

Loss

The day he moved out was terrible —
That evening she went through hell.
His absence wasn't a problem
But the corkscrew had gone as well.

Wendy Cope

The Long Finish

Decades later, I can barely remember
the house or even what room – a kitchen
I suspect, that first or last place, perhaps.

I know who I was with – or think I do.
We are long since parted, happily or
unhappily; it may not matter. Now,

more years have gone than are to come.
What was there once, has gone. I am not sad.
It is not over. Moving into the light

I see the bottle pour its few fat drops.
Our glasses gently touch, and one last time,
I taste whatever wine it was we drank.

Jonathan Davidson

Vintage

In a good year, the grape's secret harvest
gathers the marrow of earthen weather
in a swollen gem close to its cryptic best:
sign and figure read by the grower.
The seasons have spun and spent their days
on the sugars of flesh, the gifts of age
to the ageing to come: a boon that stays
in its change, a book that grows a new page.
The human hand that tends the vine is all
and nothing in this more-than-human art,
but raises the glass when the year is poured
for the fume of its truth to be savoured,
when the past and the present play their part.
With time unsealed at our lips we recall
what we have unworded: loss, bliss, a god.

Gregory Leadbetter

Drinking alone under the moon

Among the blossoms waits a jug of wine.
I pour myself a drink, no loved one near.
Raising my cup, I invite the bright moon
and turn to my shadow. We are now three.

But the moon doesn't understand drinking
and my shadow follows my body like a slave.
For a time moon and shadow will be my companions,
a passing joy that should last through the spring.

I sing and the moon just wavers in the sky;
I dance and my shadow whips around like mad.
While lucid still, we have such fun together!

But stumbling drunk, each staggers off alone.
Bound forever, relentless we roam:
reunited at last on the distant river of stars.

Li Bai (701 – 762)
translated by David Bowles

The wedding guests

Who knows which side of the family
he was on, only that he arrived late
with uninvited guests in tow, and before
nightfall the hotel bar was drunk dry.

Rose petals turned with a vinegar blush,
the borrowed music of the covers band
souring, empty glasses stacking like grudges,
the wedding feast now bones and crumbs.

But what we recall after is the transformation –
his miraculous laughter, the gobsmacked
guests, the hours of summer rain converted
to sugar and alcohol, stoppered with resin,

poured from clay vessels like a blessing. The best wine,
saved to last; the sweet draught of good things to come.

Jane Commane